W9-CIJ-327

COLUMBUS DISCOVERS AMERICA

COLORING BOOK

by Peter Copeland

Dover Publications, Inc.
NEW YORK

Introduction

CHRISTOPHER COLUMBUS was one of history's greatest sailors and explorers. At the end of his famous first voyage to America in 1492 he believed that he had discovered a western route across the Atlantic to the legendary lands of Asia—Japan, China and India—known to Europeans from the tales of Marco Polo, who had traveled through Asia, including China, from 1271 to 1295.

In fact, Columbus was probably not the first European to see the New World. Evidence indicates that Leif Eriksson reached it ca. 1001. But his Vinland, wherever it may have been, was not successfully settled and the venture made little impression on Europe. It was Columbus, sailing much farther south, who began the spectacular story of European discovery, exploitation and settlement in the Western Hemisphere.

Columbus came to the New World in error. Because he made a mistake in estimating the diameter of the earth, he arrived at calculations showing the earth to be smaller than it actually is, calculations that led him to believe that, from the European coast, Japan and Asia lay directly across the Western (Atlantic) Ocean. It was not until Columbus had returned to the New World on successive voyages that he finally realized that he had discovered a new continent, previously undreamed of by the wise men and geographers of Europe.

This is the story of Christopher Columbus and the men who set forth upon what is perhaps the most famous of all voyages of discovery—the discovery of America.

Peter Copeland

To Kimberly Swensen.

Copyright © 1988 by Dover Publications, Inc.
All rights reserved under Pan American and
International Copyright Conventions

Published in Canada by General Publishing Company, Ltd.,
30 Lesmill Road, Don Mills, Toronto, Ontario.
Published in the United Kingdom by Constable and Company, Ltd.

Columbus Discovers America Coloring Book is a new work,
first published by Dover Publications, Inc., in 1988.

DOVER *Pictorial Archive* SERIES

This book belongs to the Dover Pictorial Archive Series. You may use the designs and illustrations for graphics and crafts applications, free and without special permission, provided that you include no more than four in the same publication or project. (For permission for additional use, please write to Dover Publications, Inc., 31 East 2nd Street, Mineola, N.Y. 11501.)

However, republication or reproduction of any illustration by any other graphic service whether it be in a book or in any other design resource is strictly prohibited.

International Standard Book Number: 0-486-25542-5

Manufactured in the United States of America
Dover Publications, Inc., 31 East 2nd Street, Mineola, N.Y. 11501

From the writings of the second-century Greek geographer Ptolemy, the scholars and wise men of Columbus' day knew that the world was round, but no one was quite sure just what lands lay on the other side of the world, or how they could be reached.

The seaport of Lisbon, 1479. The Portuguese, led by Prince Henry the Navigator (1394–1460), became the first great medieval world explorers. In 1488, Portuguese ships rounded the Cape of Good Hope, at the southern tip of Africa, and, in 1498, six years after Columbus made his first voyage to the west, Vasco da Gama reached India by sailing east around Africa.

Christopher Columbus was born in the great Italian seaport of Genoa in 1451. As a young sailor he became convinced that it was possible to reach Asia by sailing west across the Atlantic, a shorter route than the one around Africa. He listened to seafarers' tales of legendary islands far out in the Western Ocean. Beyond these, he believed, lay China and the lands of the Far East.

After many efforts, in 1486 Columbus was finally granted an audience with Ferdinand and Isabella, King and Queen of Spain. He urged them to finance a voyage of discovery to open the far-off lands of Asia to Spanish trade.

A sixteenth-century carved altarpiece shows Ferdinand and Isabella entering Granada after the siege of 1492. With the fall of the city, a Moslem stronghold, Ferdinand and Isabella united Spain under Christian rule. It was after this triumph that the monarchs at last had time to interest themselves in Columbus and his enterprise. They ordered ships, men and supplies to be provided to their new admiral for his proposed exploration.

The *Santa María* was Columbus' flagship on his first voyage of discovery. A square-rigged merchant ship of about 100 tons, she carried a crew of about 40 men and boys.

The *Niña* (in the distance) and *Pinta* (in the foreground) were caravels—smaller merchant ships. For the trip across the Western Ocean, both were altered to be rigged with square sails. They carried crews of 24 and 26 men respectively.

At the southern Spanish seaport of Palos, the ships of Columbus, on royal orders, loaded stores and supplies and signed on crews.

The sailors of Columbus' day believed that, far out in the vastness of the unknown sea, lived great sea serpents able to attack and destroy ships. A Swedish "observer" recorded sighting a great sea snake that "puts up his head on high like a pillar and catches away men and devours them."

9

The three ships set out from Palos on the morning of August 3, 1492, bound for the Canary Islands, Spanish possessions off the coast of West Africa. During their last days on shore the sailors made their confessions in church and took Holy Communion.

Arriving at Grand Canary Island, repairs and alterations were made. The rudder of the *Pinta* was replaced and the *Niña* was rerigged to carry square sails.

On September 6, 1492, the ships of Columbus set out across the Western Ocean. The admiral set his course to the westward, bound, he believed, for the far-off mainland of Asia.

The wind blew steadily for days on end and the weather remained fine, "like that of Andalusia in April," Columbus wrote. On the night of September 15 a meteor with a flaming tail flashed across the sky, alarming the sailors, who thought it was an omen of bad luck.

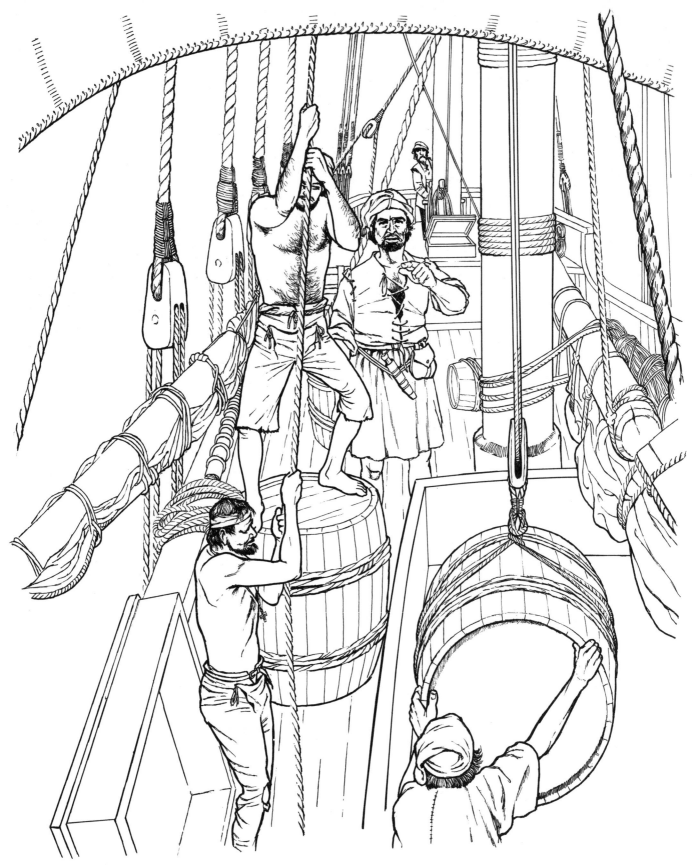

The sailors stood "watch and watch"—four hours on watch and four hours off. When they were not on watch, the men handled sails, worked aloft, swabbed decks and did many other necessary jobs. Having no beds or sleeping area aboard the crowded ship, they would curl up, perhaps in a coil of mooring line under the ship's bows, to get what sleep they could before being called out on deck again for their next watch. In fair weather the men could count on one hot meal a day, usually a stew made of salt meat or fish with rice, beans and, perhaps, garlic.

As the fine weather continued, day after day, the men of the morning watch often discovered flying fish that had come aboard during the night. They were promptly appropriated for the stew pot.

Columbus was an experienced seaman and navigator. Here he takes a sun sight with a mariner's quadrant, the only instrument of navigation he ever used to fix his position. Although it is not a very accurate instrument, the quadrant, together with the compass, were what the admiral depended on to find his position and sailing direction.

Another device that assisted the ship master was the sounding lead and line. A cylinder of lead was attached to a line. When it was thrown into the water, an experienced sailor could tell the depth of the water through which the ship was passing. Greased with tallow, the lead picked up a sample of the ocean floor. A muddy, pebbled or sandy bottom could sometimes help a navigator ascertain that he was nearing land. But the lead was of little use far out in the open ocean, where the depth of water might be as much as 14,000 feet.

As the days passed, the sailors began to grumble that they were venturing too far upon the unknown sea—that the fair winds which propelled them would prevent them from ever returning to Spain. But, by chance, the winds shifted, allaying their fears, and the admiral calmed them with his confidence and "soft words."

One of the sailors' favorite recreations was fishing. When the ships entered the Sargasso Sea, an area where the ocean surface was filled with floating seaweed, the men caught tuna and dolphin—a welcome addition to their diet of salted and dried food.

At sunset on October 7, Columbus ordered a change in course to west-southwest, in order to follow the passage of a great flock of birds flying in that direction. The admiral believed that following the birds would bring him to land. It is possible that, had he not changed course, the ships would have been caught in the Gulf Stream and wrecked on the coast of Florida.

The sailors were cheered by the sight of so many birds, some of which they thought they recognized as land birds. Surely, they thought, Asia must lie just over the horizon.

As the days passed, the sailors saw more and more evidence that land was near. On October 11, they saw pieces of wood floating in the water, one of which bore fresh leaves.

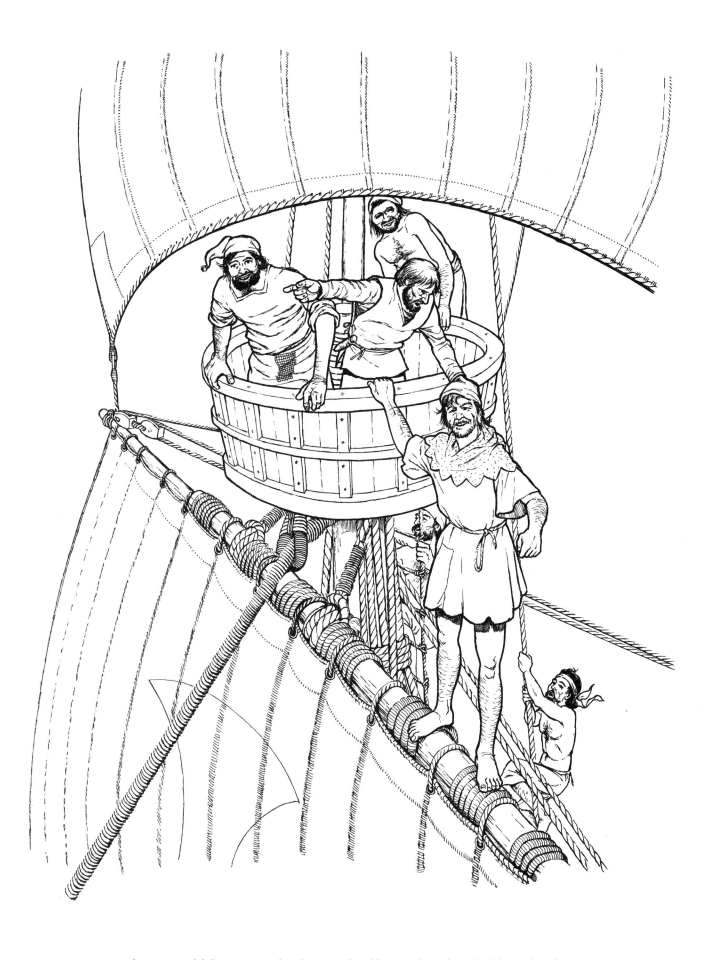

After several false reports, land was sighted by a sailor, identified by Columbus as
Rodrigo de Triana, aboard the *Pinta* on the night of October 11, 1492.

The three ships sailed around the island called Guanahaní in the Bahamas until they found an anchorage on the morning of October 12. Columbus and his officers, carrying the royal flag of Spain and the banner of Ferdinand and Isabella, went ashore on the day of discovery, sank to their knees on the beach and gave thanks to God for their safe arrival.

The native islanders stared at the strange ships of Spain, the most remarkable
sight they had ever seen.

Columbus gave the island the name of San Salvador. The islanders were of the
Arawak nation. Columbus called them Indians in the belief that they were
inhabitants of the Indian subcontinent of Asia. The admiral described them as a
gentle, friendly and trusting people.

The Spanish sailors were to learn many things from the Indians. They were amazed to discover the Indians smoking cigars made of rolled tobacco leaves. They inserted them into their noses, lighted them and inhaled the smoke. The men of Europe had never before seen tobacco or encountered the habit of smoking.

After exploring San Salvador, the Spaniards seized several of the islanders and took them along by force when they sailed away. Columbus believed that the island was one of a group that lay off the coast of Asia. The Spaniards demanded that the captives guide the ships to a nearby island where they had heard gold might be found.

On October 14 the ships sailed to the southwest, sighting a number of islands of the Bahamas and visiting several, always questioning the islanders about gold. On October 28, the ships arrived at the island of Cuba, which the admiral believed to be Japan. Trading with the Indians, the Spaniards exchanged beads and articles of clothing for fresh fruit and vegetables, but discovered no gold.

Having spent some time exploring Cuba, Columbus, aboard the *Santa María*, pondered his charts. After attempts to question the Indians who had come to trade with the strange white men, he guessed that he might at last have arrived at China.

On their travels through the islands, the Spaniards heard frightening tales from the friendly Indians about the fierce cannibal Caribs, a warrior people who raided the islands and carried off men, women and children, whom they enslaved—many of whom they cooked and ate. The Caribs painted their bodies in stripes and designs. Some of the men wore their hair on one half of their heads, shaving the other half.

On December 5, still searching for the mainland of Asia, the ships of discovery arrived off the coast of Haiti, called Española by Columbus. Here, at last, the Spaniards discovered gold, worn as ornaments by the natives of the island.

On Christmas Eve, the *Santa María* went aground on a coral reef off the coast of Haiti. The local Indians helped the admiral and his men to salvage whatever could be brought ashore.

With the loss of the *Santa María*, Columbus realized that he had to return to Spain. The Spaniards built a stockaded fort at Española and left a garrison of sailors who were happy to stay on the island and search for gold. On January 2, 1493, the men had a farewell party ashore and, on January 4, Columbus set sail on the long voyage back to Spain aboard the *Niña*, his new flagship.

Stopping for the night at a secluded anchorage, the *Niña* and *Pinta* sent a boat ashore to pick up fresh supplies of food. Here the Spaniards had their first fight with hostile Indians. In the skirmish, two of the Indians were wounded and their companions retreated into the forest.

On January 16, 1493, the wind being favorable, Columbus set a course across the open ocean for Spain. For many days the weather remained fine and the two small ships made excellent time.

On the night of February 14, a storm separated the two ships and great waves swept across their decks, nearly swamping them. The next morning, Columbus could see no sign of the *Pinta*. The *Niña* struggled through the storm, which lasted two days. When the weather at last cleared, the sailors of the *Niña* spotted land on the horizon.

On February 18, the *Niña* anchored at the Portuguese island of Santa Maria in the Azores. The admiral sent a party of sailors ashore to give thanks to God for their safe arrival. The sailors were detained by the Portuguese governor of the island, but were later released to return to the *Niña*.

In the first days of March, having left the Azores, the *Niña* sailed through another great storm that almost wrecked the little ship along the rocky coast of Portugal. On March 4, the *Niña* anchored at Rastelo, in the outer harbor of Lisbon. Columbus sent a letter telling of his discoveries to the King and Queen of Spain, and was invited to visit the King of Portugal.

On March 13, the *Niña* sailed from Lisbon and, two days later, anchored at her home port of Palos. Just a few hours later, the *Pinta* rejoined her sister ship. Having survived the storm, she had sailed for home on a different route.

The letter the admiral had sent to Ferdinand and Isabella arrived at the royal court at Barcelona. At the end of April, Columbus was received with honor by the monarchs at the alcazar, where the court saw the assembled wonders, including captive Indians, that the admiral had brought home to Spain from the New World.

Although he later realized his error, at the end of this famous achievement, the great voyage of discovery, Columbus still believed that he had explored the islands that lay off the coast of Asia. He was to make three more trips to the New World before his death in 1506.

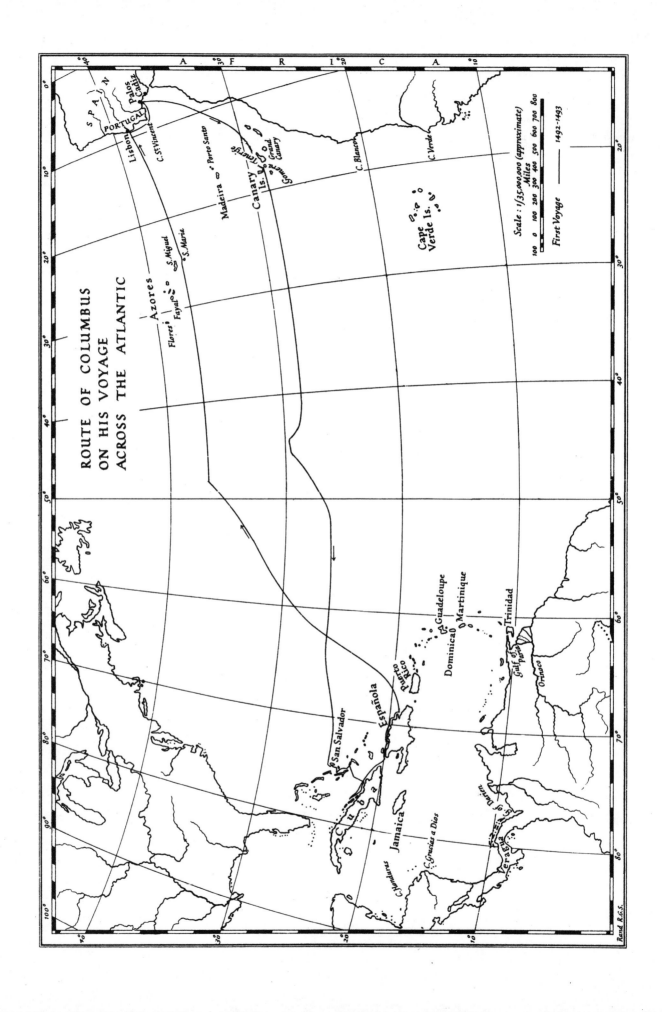

ROUTE OF COLUMBUS
ON HIS VOYAGE
ACROSS THE ATLANTIC